A Note to Parents and Teachers

Dorling Kindersley Readers is a compelling reading programme for children, designed in conjunction with leading literacy experts, including Cliff Moon M.Ed., Honorary Fellow of the University of Reading. Cliff Moon has spent many years as a teacher and teacher educator specializing in reading and has written more than 140 books for children and teachers. He reviews regularly for teachers' journals.

Beautiful illustrations and superb full-colour photographs combine with engaging, easy-to-read stories to offer a fresh approach to each subject in the series. Each *Dorling Kindersley Reader* is guaranteed to capture a child's interest while developing his or her reading skills, general knowledge, and love of reading.

The four levels of *Dorling Kindersley Readers* are aimed at different reading abilities, enabling you to choose the books that are exactly right for your child:

Level 1 – Beginning to read
Level 2 – Beginning to read alone
Level 3 – Reading alone
Level 4 – Proficient readers

The "normal" age at which a child begins to read can be anywhere from three to eight years old, so these levels are intended only as a general guideline.

No matter which level you select, you can be sure that you are helping children learn to read, then read to learn!

Dorling **DK** Kindersley

LONDON, NEW YORK, MUNICH,
PARIS, MELBOURNE, DELHI

Project Editor Deborah Lock
Art Editor C. David Gillingwater
Senior Art Editor Clare Shedden
Production Shivani Pandey
Picture Researcher Marie Osborn
Jacket Designer Karen Burgess
Indexer Lynn Bresler

Reading Consultant
Cliff Moon M.Ed.

Published in Great Britain by Dorling Kindersley Limited
80 Strand, London WC2R 0RL

2 4 6 8 10 9 7 5 3

Copyright © 2001 Dorling Kindersley Limited, London
A Penguin Company

A CIP catalogue record for this book is
available from the British Library.

ISBN 0-7513-2911-8

Colour reproduction by Colourscan, Singapore
Printed and bound in China by L Rex Printing Co., Ltd.

The publisher would like to thank the following for
their kind permission to reproduce their images:
t=top, b=bottom, l=left, r=right, c=centre

Bridgeman Art Library, London / New York:
Giraudon 32cr. **Corbis UK Ltd:** Front jacket, 2tr,
2br, 20br, 30tc, 31. **Ecoscene:** 22cb; Peter Hillme 24.
Mary Evans Picture Library: 32tl. **Robert Harding
Picture Library:** 3, 15, 16tr, 16-17; Vulcan 15. **N.H.P.A.:**
Brian Hawks 27. **Oxford Scientific Films:** Anne Head 14.
Pa Photos: 4. **Planet Earth Pictures:** 13, 19c, 23tc;
Dorian Wiesel 29. **Science Photo Library:** 5;
David Halpern 25; NASA 32br; Peter Ryan 26.
Frank Spooner Pictures: 9. **Tony Stone Images:**
Back jacket, 7. **Topham Picturepoint:** 12tc, 18bc, 32cl.

see our complete
catalogue at

www.dk.com

DORLING KINDERSLEY *READERS*

Eruption!

THE STORY OF VOLCANOES

Written by Anita Ganeri

A Dorling Kindersley Book

What looks like a mountain
but spits out fire?
What shoots clouds of smoke
from a hole in its top?
What sometimes explodes
with a BANG?

A volcano!
It's starting to erupt.

The story of a volcano
starts underground.
If you jump up and down
on the ground,
it feels solid and hard.

But inside the earth,
it is so hot that the rocks melt.
The rocks are runny
like melted butter.

Melted rock
Inside a volcano,
the melted rock rises
because it is hotter
and lighter than the
rocks around it.

Melted
rock

Sometimes the melted rock
bursts up through a hole
or a crack in the ground.
This is how a volcano begins.

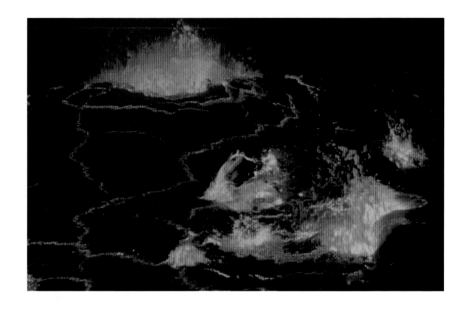

The rock that comes out of a volcano is called lava. At first, it is runny and red-hot. It cools down in the air and turns into hard, black rock.

Cooled lava

Some volcanoes spurt out
fiery fountains of lava.
Other volcanoes pour out lava
in great rivers of fire.
Once the lava starts flowing,
nothing can stop it.
It can bury whole villages
and set trees and
houses on fire.

Volcanoes have different shapes
and sizes.
Some volcanoes erupt with a bang.
Hot rocks and ash
shoot high into the air.
These volcanoes form
cone-shaped mountains
with steep sides.

Other volcanoes erupt quietly.
The lava oozes gently out of the top
and spreads out all around.
These volcanoes are low and wide.

The biggest volcano
Mauna Loa in
Hawaii is the biggest
volcano in the world.
It is an amazing
5,486 metres high.

Some volcanoes erupt violently.
They blast out
clouds of hot ash and dust.
The ash is made of
tiny pieces of lava.
The ash and dust
shoot high into the air.
Some of it lands near the volcano.
It covers buildings and fields
in thick, dark grey powder.

Some ash and dust is carried away
by the wind.
It can block out the sun and
turn day into night.

At the top of a volcano
is a hollow called a crater.
In it is a hole called the vent.
Lava, ash and dust
come out of the vent.
Some craters are huge and
can be many kilometres wide.

When a volcano stops erupting,
the crater is left.
Some old craters fill up with water
to form huge lakes.
Sometimes the crater becomes
a dry, grassy plain.

Extinct volcanoes

We call a volcano that has stopped erupting 'extinct'. It will probably never erupt again.

When a volcano shoots out lava
and ash, we say that it is erupting.
We call a volcano
that is erupting 'active'.
Kilauea in Hawaii is
the most active volcano
on earth.
It has erupted non-stop
since 1983!

We call a volcano that is not
erupting 'dormant'.
That means it is sleeping,
but it could erupt at any time.
Montserrat is a tiny island
in the Caribbean Sea.
It used to be a beautiful place
to live.
Then, in 1995, a volcano called
Chance's Peak started to erupt.

It had been dormant for 400 years.
Many people had to leave
their homes as ash fell everywhere.
Some left the island
and went to live
in another country.
It was too dangerous
for them to stay.

Volcanic ash

Mount Vesuvius is a volcano
in Italy.
In AD 79, Mount Vesuvius
erupted violently, blasting hot ash
and gas into the air.
The ash buried the town
of Pompeii and
thousands of people died.
Today, people have cleared
the ash away.
You can walk around
the streets of Pompeii and
see the Roman ruins.

*A cast of a dog
covered by the ash.*

The ruins of the Roman town of Pompeii

Pumice stone

Pumice stone is a type of lava. It is used for rubbing away hard skin. It is the only type of rock that floats.

Volcanoes can be useful.

On the slopes of volcanoes, the soil is good for growing crops.

In some places, blocks of solid lava are used to build roads, bridges and houses. Precious gold and diamonds are found in some volcanic rock.

Near a volcano,
the underground rocks get very hot.
The hot rocks heat up water,
which turns to steam.
Sometimes a giant jet
of boiling water and steam
bursts up through the ground
and into the air.
The jet is called a geyser.

Hot water

In some countries,
people use hot
underground water to
heat their homes and
make electricity.

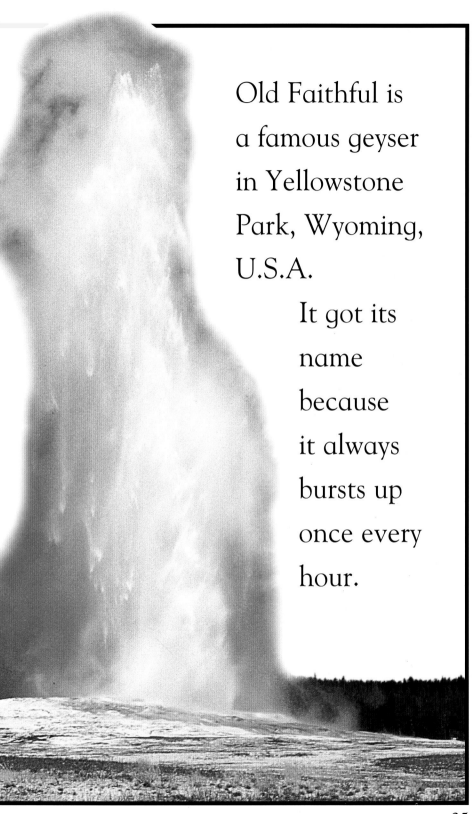

Old Faithful is a famous geyser in Yellowstone Park, Wyoming, U.S.A. It got its name because it always bursts up once every hour.

There are lots of volcanoes
under the sea.
You can't see most of them.
But some underwater volcanoes
are so tall that they poke up
from the sea to make islands.

In 1963, a volcano erupted
under the sea near Iceland.
The sea started to smoke and steam.
By the next day,
the volcano had grown and
a brand-new island had formed.
The local people called it Surtsey,
named after an
Icelandic fire god.

Hawaii is a group of more than
100 islands in the Pacific Ocean.
The islands are the tops
of huge underwater volcanoes.
Some of these volcanoes have
two or more craters,
but they erupt very gently.

In some places,
lava flows into the sea and
makes it hiss and steam.
Some of the beaches have
black sand, which is made from
crushed-up lava.

Volcanologists are scientists
who try to find out
how volcanoes work.
They want to know when volcanoes
are going to erupt so that
people living nearby
can be moved to safety.

But volcanologists have not found all the answers yet.
No one knows when a volcano will erupt – until it actually does!

Volcano Facts

There are about 1,500 active volcanoes on earth. About 50 of them erupt every year, but most of these eruptions happen underwater.

In 1883, the volcano on the island of Krakatoa in Indonesia erupted with the loudest bang ever heard.

The word 'volcano' comes from Vulcan, the Roman god of fire.

Mount St. Helens is a volcano in Washington, U.S.A. It erupted in 1980 after being dormant for 123 years. The blast blew 8,000 million tons of rock off the top.

The biggest volcano in the universe is Olympus Mons on Mars. It stands an amazing 27 kilometres high. It last erupted 200 million years ago and is now extinct.